Reviews

Blood Related: Tomorrow Never Came gave me a unique emotional ride through the eyes of the characters in this story. The main characters are family members challenged with raising children in a community where they are likely to fall prey to negative influences without the nurturing of this tight-knit family. Gregory Davis' ability to navigate the reader through expressions of love, concern, jealousy, and covetousness presents a story that keeps the reader intrigued, engaged and charged with the reality that sometimes a strong family isn't enough...."
—**Charles Boyce Jr., Attorney**

"If you are looking to initiate a discussion centered on unresolved trauma, *Blood Related: Tomorrow Never Came* is a great place to start. Gregory Davis' display of raw unapologetic emotion causes you to be drawn into every word, which invites a "trauma bond" that you might share with him regarding your own unresolved trauma issues."
—**Sgt. Willie C. Davis, Pulaski County Sheriff's Department/OK Program Facilitator**

"Greg has created a tough-minded, thought-provoking character in *Blood Related: Tomorrow Never Came.* He keeps the reader engaged by combining intrigue, the struggle for power, and the fragility of a family dynamic."
—**Ian Nickla, LMSW/Youth Leader**

"A gripping and superb drama, that keeps you in suspense throughout the reading. It's fast-paced and will keep you wanting more. It definitely speaks to fatherlessness in our urban communities."
—**Susan Madison, Retired Counselor**

Blood Related

blood related

tomorrow never came

gregory d. davis

Blood Related
© 2021 Gregory D. Davis

ISBN: 978-1-7350965-2-0
All rights reserved

All rights reserved. No part of this publication may be reproduced, distributed, or transmitted in any form or by any means, including photocopying, recording, or other electronic or mechanical methods without the prior written permission of the publisher, except in the case of brief quotation embodied in critical reviews and certain other non-commercial uses permitted by copyright law.

For permission requests, email the publisher, addressed: "Attention Permission Coordinator," at the following address:

Samone Publishing
infodrsamonebrown@gmail.com

samonepublishing.com

Dedication

I dedicate this book to the memory of my dearly departed mother, Ms. Henrie Lee Davis. To my nephew, Mr. Christopher Dwayne Davis, whose life ended way too soon. Finally, to my childhood friend, Mr. Aharanwa Captolore Smith.

I will always cherish your memories in my heart.

Acknowledgments

First, I thank my Lord and Savior for blessing me to share this story with the readers of this book. Without Him, none of this would be possible. I'd like to thank my family and friends who supported my project by providing content and candid feedback. I also thank the readers of this book, of which I hope they will find it to be entertaining and thought provoking.

This adventure is the start of many more to come, and I plan on enjoying the ride.

Disclaimer

This is a true story. The events depicted in this book took place in Little Rock, Arkansas, in the late '90s, and early 2000s. Out of respect for the survivors, the names have been changed. Out of respect for the dead, the rest has been told exactly as it occurred.

Foreword

According to the Centers for Disease Control (CDC), homicide is the leading cause of death for African American males, ages 10-35. Firearms account for almost 80% of all homicides. While most black people are aware of America's long history with violence and guns, one rarely anticipates being affected personally by its sting. Neither do we imagine the residual trauma that escorts itself into the lives of mothers, fathers, sisters, and brothers.

In this case, it is a beloved uncle. An uncle who delves into the many nuances that often lend itself to the fatal consequences that often impact our African American communities and families.

No one is exempt from the unresolved trauma residue that may lay dormant, deep inside of our being. Especially when for some strange reason, life wakes it up. In *Blood Related*, author Gregory Davis shatters the camouflage and reveals his heartfelt presentation. It is reminiscent of Marvin Gaye's 70s' title song, "What's Going On?" I am certain that his intentional, yet emotional presentation of a life that did not get the benefit of experiencing "tomorrow," because it never came, will nudge your inner-most emotions of anger and sadness. Society has ingrained these feelings in black families and communities for a long time.

I honorably introduce you to an emotional read. And I recommend a quiet space and a box of Kleenex®.
—**Sgt. Willie C. Davis/Pulaski County Sheriff's Department**

Introduction

Some families function from a distance, while others operate with extreme dysfunction. Almost every family has that one element that makes them close, although others interact from places full of secrets, scandal, and mystery. If it is "good and pleasant for brethren to dwell together in unity," how much more should one's family do so?

The crazy fact about family secrets and the driving force behind family dissent, is everybody knows, yet no one talks about the thing that drives a wedge between everyone. Take, for instance, that one aunt who is not really an aunt, but a mother who abandoned her baby and who allowed "Big Momma," to play mother. Or perhaps that uncle who everyone avoided, and watched around the kids, because the young flesh of his nieces and nephews attracted his hands. Yes, those family secrets.

Yet, this is not one of those family enigmas. This is a narrative of how blood can become soured. How kin can turn on kin. This is tantamount to the Bible's Cain and Abel, the lack of civility displayed by the Union North of the Confederate South; brother against brother. These are confidences which the entire family knows.

The world would receive him on a cold, windy day on February 7, 1976: Christopher Dewayne Davis. He was born a child of promise and of strength, and he occupies a world out of place with its own humanity. Yet, for the Davis family, this bundle of joy would become a son, brother, grandson, and nephew. He would grow to be the family's heartbeat until early, one hot summer in 2002, when the beating of his heart would cease, due to a murderous bullet from an assassin.

A motive would be unknown to the world. Local law enforcement would label his death as a cold case, but despite the designation or reasoning others might use for not solving Christopher's murder, there were no suspicions among kin. The greatest evidence would soon emanate from the hearts of those most familiar with Christopher's comings and goings; his family.

Although Chris' death left a hole in the hearts of his immediate relatives, it would create a larger one with those further out, yet connected by blood.

CHAPTER 1

Nephew

Chris was born to an 18-year-old, unwed mother, on February 7, 1976. Loraine, his mother, my sister, was a carefree teenager, who was caring and like a mother to me. She stepped in for our mother, Ella Mae Davis, when she had to work a second shift on her job. Loraine had no idea about motherhood, but was more like a mother to me, rather than my oldest sister.

I was next to the youngest out of six children. I had a younger sister, Taylor, but Chris was like the little brother I never had. In the early years, Chris was the little nephew who always wanted to hang around his uncles, especially Uncle Willie.

Willie was always welcoming with Chris, and his desire to hang around him wasn't a bother. He was a high school football player and Chris loved going to the games to watch his uncle play.

There's a 1982 photo of Chris and Willie after a "Turkey Day" game between rivals Little Rock Central High and the Hall High Warriors. The picture made the local newspaper, and Chris was ecstatic that he was in a photo with his uncle. The following year, Willie left Little Rock to attend the University of Central Arkansas, in Conrad, Arkansas.

We all lived in a three-bedroom house in the inner city of Little Rock. Our mother, Chris' grandmother, was a single parent as well, who provided for the entire household. Our mother was loving. She was short in stature, but strong in words and meaning. She was nurturing and all about family. Above all, she was intelligent, and she loved the Lord.

Mother was passionate about us doing what was right and making sound choices and decisions. Chris grew up a mild-mannered child. He was a joy to be around. He had wit, and he knew what he wanted when it came down to his time with Uncle Willie, when he visited from college during holiday breaks.

Once, a young lady my brother dated, came to visit at our mother's house. Unbeknownst to my brother, the young lady interrupted the time Chris wanted to spend with his uncle.

In my brother's presence, Chris asked the young lady, "When are you going to leave?"

He didn't realize he was being rude, as he was only doing what kids do. My brother gently admonished him, but understood he meant no harm. He only wanted his time with his uncle.

My older brothers believed I couldn't keep up with them. They wouldn't allow me to participate in certain activities. Therefore, they always left me behind. As a result, Chris and I became close. We were nine years apart, and throughout the neighborhood, I protected him as if he were my little brother. My brothers and I made sure we were a positive influence in his life.

Our childhoods were uneventful for the most part. We didn't have much, but we had each other. We were a strong, close-knit family. My mother was a praying woman and a believer in God. She raised us in church; almost every time the doors were open, you would find us at Antioch Baptist Church in College Station, Arkansas.

Chris was an excellent student in school, and in time, he became involved in sports. He excelled in football and basketball. In 1982, my sister gave birth to another son, Reginald (Reggie) and also gave birth to a daughter, Katelyn, two years later. By the time they were born, my sister no longer lived with us. They moved to the other side of town known as Southwest Little Rock. That area was pretty shady and we didn't care for the kids to grow up there. Later, we discovered she used drugs. As the years went by, I left for college.

I followed Willie to the University of Central Arkansas and didn't see my nephew as much until I'd come home to visit. My mother kept me updated on various situations that went on at home. Notably, there was an obvious change in the behavior of my oldest sister, and my mother knew it. She could tell she had gotten deeper into her drug use and it affected the kids, especially Chris. Mother was more concerned about him because he was older and there was a "gap" in the attention he needed to keep him headed in the right direction.

I often talked to Chris in an attempt to figure out what was going on with him. Through our conversations, I could tell he was migrating to the streets. We were away, and the lure of cash and drugs tugged at him. He tried to fight it off, because he still visited my mother's house, and didn't want her to know what was going on with him.

It got to a point where Chris was in and out of the house, and my mother could not control his behavior. He disappeared for days at a time, and that caused concern for his safety. Willie was now an officer with the local police department and he discovered Chris had a juvenile pick up order out on him. However, no one knew his whereabouts.

Once, they dispatched Willie on a loitering call concerning a group of young black males hanging out at a housing project. When he approached the group of teens, he didn't recognize Chris at first.

He then heard one teen say, "That's Chris D's uncle. He's not going to bother him."

Willie pretended he didn't hear the comment as he scanned the crowd again. He saw Chris sitting alone in silence, off to himself. They made brief eye contact, and he asked his partner to put Chris in the front seat of his squad car. Although the detention center was only a few minutes away from the location, he stated that was the longest drive he'd ever experienced. Neither one of them spoke one word. By that time, it was evident Chris had chosen the streets and his social situation didn't help the matter.

As time went on, Chris became a major player in the drug game, and his mother became one of the drug game's most reliable customers.

CHAPTER 2

Street Life

In Chris' mind, people's expectations of him consisted of too many rules and regulations. He could no longer live under his grandmother's roof and partake in the street life as well. He was all in with the drug game.

Chris hung around a group of wayward youngsters. According to rumors, they affiliated with a gang and dealt drugs. He also regularly skipped school. Teachers and school leadership notified my mother of his truancy. She tried to address it through many parent-teacher meetings, but they were unsuccessful. Chris spiraled down the wrong path. He later gave up on school altogether and made the street life his destiny.

A guy by the name of Meeko was the kingpin on the streets. People knew him as a ruthless individual who only cared about his bottom line. He was a stocky guy, who had one leg because someone blew his kneecap off during an altercation. The incident laid him up and put him out of action for quite some time. Later he re-emerged on the scene to exact revenge on those responsible for his handicap. That's when he developed his ruthless reputation. Once, Meeko went to the funeral of the mother of someone who owed him money. He walked up to the casket as if he were paying last respects and took expensive jewelry off of the body. His action sent a message to the family that he was serious and wanted that debt settled.

However, Meeko was also like a hero to the kids in the projects because of the gifts and treats he gave them whenever he came around. Other times, he sponsored picnics or sporting activities.

Still, Meeko was on the radar of law enforcement for several unsolved murders and assaults. He got off on many charges because "the streets don't talk." His lieutenants also recruited minors to commit crimes or take the rap for his crimes, in exchange for recognition and "street cred."

Chris desired to get Meeko's attention by volunteering to hit some "licks" for him. He started out by robbing neighborhood convenience stores. Once, Chris pistol-whipped an elderly man for moving slowly when he opened the register during a robbery. Authorities later charged him with robbing the houses of some of the wealthy people in West Little Rock. These were prominent, high-profile folks who used drugs and didn't want their names logged in police reports or in the news. They also refused to file any reports for fear of retaliation. The results of the assignments pleased Meeko. Chris graduated to robbing rival drug dealers who had set up shop in their territory.

Meeko's main rival was a thug who went by the name of "Cutty." He was flashy, wanted to be seen as having it going on, and predictable. Cutty acted tough and talked big, but would always show his true colors whenever someone called his bluff. He got the name "Cutty" for being cut-throat on the streets. Yet, he would snitch you out to save his own skin. He was a small guy, with a big mouth. Meeko and Cutty both came up through the ranks together, but a dispute over a girl ended their relationship.

Skylar was Cutty's longtime girlfriend who met Meeko at the State Fair when Cutty served time on a drug charge. She was beautiful and innocent with long, black, curly hair. Yet, she was a homebody. She seldom ventured out to the streets. Skylar was never out in the clubs and she didn't do things that weren't ladylike. She was smart, but she made poor decisions when it came to dating. Skylar had a penchant for the knuckle-headed type. Meeko knew Cutty had a main love interest in Skylar, but never met her. Cutty asked him to take care of his disabled mother and his girlfriend by giving them money every month. Meeko would usually send a soldier to make the monthly drop, but decided one month to do it himself. He met Skylar at the house of Cutty's mother. The introduction wasn't lengthy. He made the drop, and Skylar walked him outside. He gave her his number and asked her to call him if she ever needed anything. Throughout Cutty's 3½ year sentence, the two of them dated off and on.

Word got back to Cutty that they were in a relationship. He never said anything to either of them about what he heard until they released him. Cutty vowed revenge on Meeko. While serving time, he made a deal with the prosecutors to turn State's evidence and work with local and federal authorities to broker a deal with a drug plant. That plant happened to work with Meeko. His name was

Omar. He was a low-level street hustler who didn't have a home life. He wasn't raised to show empathy. When you looked into his eyes, you saw nothing but emptiness. Omar wore a curl and many thin, gold chains. He wanted to look the part of a kingpin, but the streets knew better. He was Meeko's right-hand man, but he felt slighted because Meeko had not given him the shot he thought he deserved to rise in the ranks and get his "corner." In his mind, Meeko dissed him in the streets and around the young soldiers in the clique.

Omar arranged for a shipment of 10 kilos, valued at $180,000, of pure cocaine to be delivered in the bottoms of the College Station community. He and Meeko were to meet with the "connect" out of Dallas. Omar knew them only as "Oak Cliff," which is a large community located in the southwest part of Dallas, known for being one of the rowdiest parts of the city.

Oak Cliff is made up of almost entirely of Blacks and Hispanics, which happened during the "White Flight" period in which the good white folks moved to the suburbs. Omar met these characters several years ago during one of his drug runs to Dallas. Meeko had a duffel bag containing $180,000 in cash for the drugs. He was unaware that over 30 DEA agents and local authorities surrounded them and waited to pounce once they received the signal to move in. After Meeko applied the testing to one block of the cocaine, and concluded it was pure "nose candy," he agreed to proceed with the transaction. That was the signal for the authorities to move in. In a New York minute, Meeko faced a lifetime in federal prison. With Meeko in lockup, with no bond, and no end in sight, Cutty retreated to anonymity, no longer having "street cred." Omar was now the main man. He had his own network and ideas of how he wanted to lead the crew. His nephew, Doby, was his right-hand man. Omar and Chris were cousins. Omar's father, Moses, was the brother of Chris' grandfather, Odell. By the time Omar had risen to power, Chris had already made his name in the streets as the go-to person for a solid connect. As Chris would ascend in the drug game, his mother's drug use would too.

Katelyn and Reggie lived with their mother, but were neglected due to her being absent. They rarely had food in the house. Chris fended for his siblings to make sure they had food and clothing. He gave his mother money to take care of those needs, but she blew it on the next hit. One night, my mother called my sister's house to check up on Katelyn and Reggie, and found out they were hungry. They told her they hadn't had a decent meal in days.

From that night on, Chris' siblings lived with my mother. After a while, she adopted them. Chris loved his grandmother with all his heart. He would never say a cross word back to her, but felt he had no other choice but to sell drugs. He attempted to give her money, but she refused the gesture. She always told him he could do better by making an honest living. He promised he would one day, but not right then. He felt the need to make quick money to do what he felt needed to be done. Those plans were altered because of a rumor being spread in the streets regarding his mother. Her drug use, and the position it put him in, already disturbed him. He confided in some acquaintances that her drug use had gotten out of hand, now that his siblings lived with his grandmother.

Chris later found that the guy he confided in was the main dealer for his mother. He was infuriated at the thought of his "homie" dealing drugs to his mother. He went over to his house and shot him multiple times, crippling him for life. They arrested him and charged him with attempted murder. He was in jail for over a year before his trial came up. The authorities sentenced him to three years in prison with time served, meaning he'd be back on the streets in six months after serving his time in a boot camp.

CHAPTER 3

Chris and Doby

Chris satisfied his obligation with the penal system and headed back to Little Rock. With no formal education or work history to fall back on, searching for a job wasn't an option. His mother used drugs while he was in, and still used them when he got out. Chris was back on the streets in Little Rock, and he looked for an opportunity to get his clientele back up. He reconnected with Omar and his nephew, Doby, whose mother was Omar's oldest sister. Doby and Chris were always cool with each other, long before they got into the drug game.

Chris got his fair share of product and hit the streets. People knew Chris and respected him on the streets as being an enforcer. He had an "I don't give a damn" attitude about things that didn't matter to him. Chris slung crack rocks to any crackhead in need. He would also "bust a cap" in anyone's ass who crossed him.

Chris moved a lot of "weight." He became the man to go to. He and Doby got close as he grinded. Chris took him under his wing and showed him the ropes of the drug game and how to survive in the streets. In return, Doby introduced Chris to some important clients. This was the opportunity Chris looked for. One particular client was a vice president of a reputable investment firm, with offices in Little Rock, New York, and California. This client would later be instrumental in keeping Chris' income flowing for some time to come.

My mother was not pleased and became more disappointed about what her oldest grandson had become. She had hoped for far better than what he'd settled for. Her foremost disappointment was knowing he'd somehow aligned himself with Omar and Doby. Although they were blood related, she didn't trust Omar and didn't want Chris associated with him. She always felt he was bad news. They grew up in the College Station community and didn't have much. Uncle Moses never married their mother, but they had several children together, with Omar being somewhere in the middle. They didn't have any family structure, and that resulted in Omar's bad reputation and rap sheet at an early age. He had been in and out of jail throughout his youth, and we never established a close relationship. His family never came to our house, and we never went to theirs.

My mother tried everything in her power to steer Chris away from the streets. She prayed day and night over him. She pleaded with him to legitimize his life, because he had a younger brother and sister who loved him, and his life choices concerned them. I and my brothers tried to stage an intervention for Chris. We tried to show him he didn't need a college education to be successful, and that there was no reward in the street life.

I eventually moved to Dallas, but I kept in constant contact with my mother and the rest of the family. I wanted a better paying job. In Little Rock, I worked a dead-end job with mediocre pay. In the "Big D," I worked in healthcare billing and coding. My brothers were in law enforcement and kept me abreast of everything going on back in Little Rock.

By this time, Chris had struck out on his own as a major player in the drug game, and Doby rode the wave with him. This relationship didn't bode well with Omar. He felt they all could thrive together in the game, but that's not what Chris wanted. Chris had established a steady and reliable stable of clientele, and a steady cash flow. He wasn't about to compromise that arrangement. He also took great care of Doby.

His high-end client continued to direct his customers to him, and they directed their friends as well. He developed a network of clients who relied on him for the good product he served. As Chris continued to rise, many low-level players wanted to be on his team. He was leery of having too many people in his circle and only trusted Doby to help him move product. The hate for his game was prevalent. Word got back to them that Omar felt some type of way that Doby worked with Chris and got assignments he would never have given him. As Chris witnessed his star continuing to rise in the drug game, he sensed the target on his back. The streets talked about it.

Chris felt the tension from some of the other street hustlers, and he felt it in his gut. He'd heard about this guy named Big D. He was a bodyguard/enforcer to the highest bidder and Chris felt he could use his services. He asked

Doby to get the word on him and see what they needed to do to get him on the team.

Big D was his name on the street, but "Mother" was his name in his "other world." He was an enforcer who stood six-foot five inches tall and weighed 280 lbs. He was a free agent of sorts, and did not belong to any one organization. His only allegiance was to whoever paid the most and for the longest period. Once someone hired him, that's who he'd work with. He wouldn't sign with more than one organization because of the conflict it would present to his personal life.

Mother's other world was an alternative lifestyle. He was gay, and enjoyed cross dressing at gay clubs around Little Rock, when he wasn't being an enforcer. It was his idea of relaxing and letting his hair down. When Mother would kick ass, the guys wouldn't retaliate because they didn't want it known that they caught a beat down from a gay guy.

The year was 1996. Chris was the ripe age of 20. In 2 ½ years, he had established himself as one of the major dealers in the entire city. He was on every major player's radar, including law enforcement. His family was at their wits' end as they tried to figure out what to do to steer him in the right direction.

By 1998, I found myself settled in Dallas. I asked my older brothers to bring Chris down with them for a visit. It wasn't only for the path Chris took, but also because of an incident that happened with Chris and my other brother. We figured a road trip would give them both the opportunity to straighten things out. I never knew if they spoke of the incident. The cause of contention wasn't clear, but I heard it involved a gun. My mother was aware and upset about the whole incident. During the visit, we put all differences aside, and all had a good time. They stayed the weekend and headed back to Little Rock the following Sunday.

    Chris liked music and often compared certain lyrics to his life. One song that was captivating to Chris was Mary J. Blige's, "My Life." As the song played, Willie recalled Chris saying that was "his song," and he sang the lyrics to the whole song. "If you look in my life and see what I've seen..." That song was encouraging and I guess he needed it during that time in his life. It always concerned him that he had to take on the responsibility of taking care of his young siblings because of his mother's choices. This put him in a situation that no young teen should have to suffer. Unfortunately, that was his way of justifying his need to enter the drug dealing arena. It would ultimately be his demise.

CHAPTER 4

Family Over Everything

It was the Easter holiday of 2001, and we had a big family gathering at my brother's house. Everyone was there. Chris brought a guest, a young lady he'd spoken about quite a few times. Her name was Jazlyn, and her daughter's name was Kendall. He seemed to really be into her. He was a different person when he was around her. She had a child, and Chris welcomed that fact and took it as a sense of responsibility to be more of a man. I found this to be a good thing and thought that maybe he was turning over a new leaf. We ate dinner and had drinks. I congratulated Chris and offered my approval of his lady friend. Not that he needed or asked for it.

I asked, "What are your plans?"

He asked, "What do you mean?"

I explained that since this young lady and her child liked him, would he leave the hustle game and get a job?

He said, "That's what I would like to do, but where can I find work with limited education?"

I offered any help I could and suggested he move to Dallas and start fresh. He welcomed that idea, but felt he'd be missing out on something if he left Little Rock. I didn't want to pressure him because he seemed relaxed and appeared happy. My mother had all her children and grandchildren together and safe, and that made her happy. They were also where she could lay eyes on them.

For a short period, Chris seemed to slowly let the dope game go. He asked about jobs in Dallas that would give him a shot. I let him know opportunities were plentiful in Dallas. All he had to do was get here. By the fall of the same year, Chris and his brother, Reggie, moved in together. Reggie graduated from barber college and they planned on investing in a barber shop. Through them moving in together, I found out Chris hadn't slowed down his dealing at all. Instead, he heightened his activity.

Reggie shared his concerns with me regarding all the traffic throughout their apartment while he was at work. He came home one evening and found a duffel bag with a lot of cash in it. The amount was $250k. This find shook Reggie to his core.

He contacted Willie, the sergeant with the Little Rock Police Department. He also contacted me. We both advised him to leave it where he found it. After observing Chris' actions for a little longer, Reggie decided to get his own place. He spoke with Chris to let him know he wasn't comfortable living there. Chris understood and assisted him in moving somewhere else. He continued to manage his operation from the first apartment.

Throughout the remainder of the year, he kept Doby busy with the connections and distribution of product. One thing concerned Doby, and that was the fact that Omar lurked around. He sent a message to Chris concerning a proposition for him. He said he had a deal that would set them both up fairly well. That might not have been bad, but Chris also used his own product. The number one rule in the drug game is don't get high off your own supply. It became noticeable to everyone who paid attention.

At the start of 2002, Chris was careless, paranoid, and not trusting of anyone in the streets except Doby. He had cut ties with Mother and was his own protector and enforcer. He didn't treat his family any differently; he always had love for his grandmother. Chris would drop by her house from time to time for a nice home-cooked meal, and the nurturing he longed for. She was the only other person he felt safe around. And he didn't feel judged whenever he was in her presence.

Chris continued to make his moves, and he stepped on toes in the process. His product wasn't as pure as it had been, and he would confront anyone who displayed displeasure in it. This didn't sit too well with Doby. Omar finally contacted Chris. He wanted to make a deal happen. It would be a partnership of sorts. They pooled their resources together, and they bought larger quantities of product. Omar was back to call certain shots, and he gave orders to Doby who wasn't fond of that, and he shared those sentiments with Chris.

I visited Little Rock on Memorial Day weekend and wanted to make sure I reached out to Chris. He was excited that I was in town and wanted me to see how he lived. He asked me to come to his apartment. I brought some beer, and we chatted. He showed me his new pit bull puppies. They were from a nice bloodline and might become a nice form of income if he bred them. Another thing Chris was proud to show me was a .45 caliber automatic pistol. The fact that he had a gun blew me away. I was also naïve to think a drug dealer wouldn't have one.

"Why do you feel the need to have such a large gun?" I asked.

He responded, "I need it for protection." I pleaded with him that whatever he was doing where he felt he needed a gun for protection, he should get out of that line of work. After visiting with other family members for the remainder of the weekend, I headed back to Dallas.

A few weeks after I returned to Dallas, Reggie called to let me know Chris had shot a young lady and almost pistol-whipped a guy to death. They were there on the pretense to buy drugs. Omar introduced those individuals to him. He vouched for them, so Chris gave them a pass and allowed them into his apartment. Once inside, they tried to rob Chris of his drugs and money. The police charged Chris and not the duo, because no one was about to report to the authorities that the situation was a drug deal gone wrong. The only weapon at the scene was the gun Chris used. The others didn't have any weapons; they tried to overpower him to take his drugs and money.

Doby had a sneaky suspicion that Omar was behind the attempted robbery. He wouldn't say anything to cause any issues until he got something solid to bring back to Chris. They charged Chris with aggravated assault and attempted murder. He was in jail for over a month before Omar posted bail. By the time the news got to me,

I tried to get in touch with Chris, to no avail. I called my mother's house.

"You just missed him," she said.

I called my niece's phone. It went to voicemail.

I spoke with Reggie, and was told Chris was over at Omar's sister's apartment. He'd been staying there since he bonded out of jail. I later left a message with Reggie to have him contact me. After a few days, Chris called.

"What happened?" I asked. He said they tried to rob him.

"Was there another way you could have handled the situation?" I pressed him for an answer.

He said he wanted to send a message, and that he remembered little of what happened because he was high. I shared my concerns about how having that gun was nothing but trouble waiting to happen. I asked about the charges he faced, and he wasn't all too sure what he was looking at in terms of the severity of charges. He said he had to find an attorney to represent him. I offered to help because I knew of an attorney who would represent him as his attorney of record. He was against that offer, because he didn't have any money for a retainer at the moment. I let him know that the attorney I knew didn't need anything at the moment because he was doing me a favor. Chris said he didn't want to owe anyone anything and that he'd figure it out and let me know.

To be exact, he didn't say the words, but I know Chris wanted to find his own attorney because he needed to gain access to money he had stashed. He didn't have anything on hand to use as a retainer; it had to be one of those "under the table deals." Plus, he didn't have anyone he felt he could trust. I know he didn't want to bring his family into danger. It was bad enough that Chris lost his apartment due to all the activity surrounding the attempted robbery. Complaints about drug activity piled up at the leasing office of his apartment complex. He was in jail for only a few months, and he lost the apartment because he did not live up to the lease agreement and the fact that there was a shooting on the premises.

I asked, "Where are you staying?" He told me he was staying at Omar's sister's place. A sense of anger, concern, and other emotions came over me. I asked, "Why are you over there? They aren't your immediate family!"

I wanted him over at my mother's house, away from them. Plus, I knew they wouldn't be running over to my mother's house because she didn't tolerate their foolishness. Chris insisted things were okay over there. His answers did not satisfy me, therefore I suggested he come to Dallas until he had a court date scheduled. He said he thought about asking me about getting away to clear his head and gather his thoughts until his next move. I felt he showed me an opening. I thought at last he saw the light. I offered to come to Little Rock to pick him up. We agreed I would come on the Fourth of July holiday. It was now the latter part of June, and we never got the chance to speak again. To be honest, I didn't feel right the last time we spoke, and I had concerns about my nephew. I sensed his life was in danger. I let him know I loved him and needed him to change his ways. But he may have resigned in his mind that things were too far gone.

CHAPTER 5

A Day of Reckoning

My mother planned a Fourth of July cookout at her house. She was extra excited that I would be in town for the festivities. Leading up to the holiday, I put in my request for the days off and tried to tie up loose ends in Dallas. I received calls from Reggie and Katelyn about how Chris was hanging with Omar and Doby quite a bit. They didn't feel that was a good thing because they knew Omar was always up to something no good.

The day before the holiday started off like any other. I called my mother for our morning conversation. We talked about her menu.

She asked, "Is there anything special you want?"

She already knew what I would say, but I said it anyway, "Macaroni and cheese!"

She shared the attendance list with me, as if it were a grand event. I guess it was in her eyes. My brothers would be there. Reggie and Katelyn were coming. My younger sister would be there. Chris would attend, according to Katelyn. My oldest sister, Chris' mother, would most likely be there. I told her I planned to leave in the morning, and should arrive around 2 p.m.

Later that night, I called my niece, Katelyn, as I do quite a bit, and she said that she spoke with Chris around 10 p.m., which happened to be the last time they talked. She and my sister were headed home from the grocery store when she thought of Chris. Katelyn called him to make sure he would still come the next day to celebrate the holiday. He had her cell phone at the time and asked what time should he arrive? She told him to be there around 2 p.m. They ended their call after confirming the time.

Sometime after that conversation, someone shot and killed Doby in West Little Rock, at the apartment complex where Chris stayed with Doby's mother and Omar. Doby and Chris were close and together all the time. Therefore, there was a lot of concern when the news broke.

Just after midnight on Wednesday morning, someone called 911 to report gunshots in West Little Rock. After answering the service call off John Barrow Road, the police found Doby's body. Someone had shot him twice in the head. No one could explain what motivated the shooting, but Chris had gone to his aunt's house earlier that evening. According to reports, it was rumored that Chris found the body. Someone also saw Chris in the area with a gun prior to the shooting. Omar was one of the first to say he saw Chris kneeling over Doby's body with a gun in his hand.

I got the news about Doby later that night, and my first question was, "Where is Chris?" No one had heard from him. The phone he borrowed from Katelyn went straight to voicemail when called. That's how the remainder of the night ended. There wasn't any concrete information, only speculation. I got a call around 9 a.m., the morning of the Fourth of July, that Chris was dead.

According to reports, a woman was driving to work in Southwest Little Rock early that morning, when the headlights of her car illuminated a pair of white sneakers protruding out of a ditch. They were the shoes of Christopher Dewayne Davis, who was deceased from a gunshot wound to the back of the neck. The local authorities didn't have any suspects, but concluded at once that it was a revenge killing, as he was a strong suspect in Doby's murder, and was the only person they looked for. I was frantic as hell and wanted to speak with someone ASAP! I called my mother's home, and my niece answered. She was uncontrollable and inconsolable. My nephew was there as well. From the background noise, I could sense the chaos and hurt the sad news brought.

******

The Fourth of July holiday morning started off uneventful. My mother milled around the house, preparing for the day's festivities. She made small talk with Taylor and Katelyn. Reggie stopped by to check in. They discussed the menu and the things they would do for the younger kids during the meal and afterwards.

There was a knock at the door. My mother could see two men through her screen door, dressed in suits and ties. They carried portfolios in their hands and they looked serious. Therefore, it concerned my mother. Katelyn answered the door.

One asked, "May we come in?"

Once inside, they stood in the living room and introduced themselves.

"I'm Detective Ray Curtis, and this is Detective Lucas Davenport," the first man said.

By that time, everyone in the house had entered the living room.

He continued, "Is this the residence of Christopher Dewayne Davis?"

My mother confirmed that it was his address. When the detectives offered their sincerest apologies, gave condolences, and informed my mother of Chris' murder, she urinated on herself right in the living room. Upon hearing the news and seeing my mother's reaction, my niece fell to her knees. My nephew did not believe what happened and went in search of answers.

He left my mother's house upset and confused about the fact that someone could shoot his brother and dump him in a ditch like yesterday's trash. He contacted some of Chris' closest friends to put a timeline together of whom he was with last and where they were last seen together. My mother knew what he attempted to do, and before he left, she pleaded with him to be careful. She didn't want any harm brought to him. She was protective of her family.

I tried to navigate my way out of Dallas for what would be one of the longest drives of my life, although it was only five hours away. A lot went through my mind, but mostly, I was angry. First, I was angry at the cowards who shot Chris in the back of the neck. Second, I was angry at Chris for putting himself in that position to be murdered in that manner. I always felt he had much promise and much to offer, but this was the way his story ended. We all tried hard to get him away from the street life, but he had to have it. How could he get careless and hang around people he knew weren't riding for him? I felt the strong desire to avenge his death.

    Evil thoughts occupied my mind as I traveled to Little Rock. When I arrived in the city, I drove down University Avenue and Roosevelt Road, and straight to my mother's house. When I pulled up, Omar was on the front porch, talking to my mother. He told her how he was out of town when he got the news that someone had killed Chris. It seemed odd, almost like he was trying to establish an alibi and convince us he had no involvement. It piqued my mother's interest, and she asked probing questions. Omar appeared nervous at the questions she asked. We talked a bit more about what happened, then he left.

    Once he was up the street and out of sight, my mother said, "He knows something!"

    I asked, "Why would you say that?"

    She said he was trying extra hard to convince her he had an alibi. She was adamant about her belief. The more I thought about it, I added things up as well. A lot of what he said seemed suspect.

    The next day, I met up with Reggie. He said he had some information to share and wanted to get in touch with the detectives. He said one of his friends saw Omar and Chris on 12th and University in the wee hours, around 3 a.m., before they discovered his body. She said Chris seemed to be high and super relaxed. He spoke to her from the passenger seat of the car. Omar was in the driver's seat, and an unknown guy was in the back seat behind Chris. That was the last time anyone saw him alive. Reggie said a couple of days before both murders, he was at his apartment with them. Chris said they needed to get more guns in the event they needed to go to war. Doby said Omar tried to get him to go to New York to pick up some product.

Doby asked, "What my country ass look like going to New York?" He said he wasn't going because he felt that the idea sounded weird. Reggie went to his apartment to cut Doby's and his kid's hair. Doby had been out all day, and when he returned, Reggie prepared to leave.

He said to Reggie, "You forgot about me!" Reggie said he'd get him tomorrow. The next day Doby was dead.

Reggie asked Doby's aunt what happened, and she said they were all talking in the apartment while she was on the phone with her boyfriend. Her boyfriend was in jail, therefore, she was attentive to the time of the call; it was 11:30 p.m.

Doby got a call from someone to get some cocaine from outside. Once he was outside, shots rang out. Omar wasn't around during the time of the shooting. His whereabouts were unknown.

Reggie came to the apartment the next day to give Chris a haircut. He saw Omar outside, talking to a group of guys. He sensed they were plotting to murder Chris. Chris was inside the apartment, alone. Reggie recalled Chris being quiet and reserved, so he left. One of Chris' closest friends called Reggie and said to make sure Chris doesn't do anything reckless. A little while later, Chris was dead. Reggie said when he plays everything back in his mind, Omar was short on Chris' money when he was in jail for shooting "that girl." Doby was handling his end, and Omar was jealous of their relationship. He felt Omar was plotting to kill Chris when he was trying to send Doby to New York, but he was in the way, therefore he had to kill him as well.

CHAPTER 6

Firecracker Fast 5K

Willie was off duty from the Little Rock Police Department when he received a call from our mother. It was a hot July morning, and he'd completed the yearly Firecracker Fast 5k road race. Her voice was shaky as she said there were some detectives at her house. They asked questions about Chris. His initial thought was, *What has he done now?*

He headed to my mother's house to see what was going on. He lived about five minutes from her. When he arrived, he noticed detectives Ray Curtis and Lucas Davenport. He knew them because they were colleagues on the force. He also knew the look in their eyes. Their eyes relayed information to him that their mouths didn't need to. As they spoke, the detectives confirmed what he had already concluded. Chris was no longer with us, murdered and tossed in a ditch next to a cemetery. How about that for irony?

After they announced Chris' violent death, a Pandora's Box of emotions, assumptions, and unverified stories flowed. We were all devastated and had to come to grips with Chris's death, however we were more torn with the notion that a close relative—a first cousin—might have had a hand in orchestrating his murder. This revelation planted a wedge between first cousins, and two brothers; my dad, Odell, and my uncle, Moses, my dad's brother. It wasn't a good feeling for any of us, but the reality was real. We managed our anger by trying to encourage and be strong for the others in the family, especially my mother.

Chris' death devastated and saddened her. It was obvious to me she would never be the same. I had never seen my mother that sad since her oldest brother, Uncle Joe, died in a tractor trailer accident in 1978. She loaded us into our station wagon and drove to Many, LA for his services. She appeared empty and lacked any desire to exist. It seemed to have taken an eternity for her to deal with his passing.

Now, here we were again, and she had the same appearance after Chris' death that she had for Uncle Joe. Chris was more her son and our younger brother, than her grandson and our nephew. He grew up in the household with us as the oldest grandchild.

She wanted to heal from the hurt of the wound in her heart. She wanted to put an end to all the questions that have haunted the family ever since that horrific moment the detectives showed up at her door. When Chris died, it felt as if someone had ripped her whole heart out of her body. She would later say that when he left, it felt like a part of her went with him. The days leading up to the funeral arrangements, my mother consumed herself with finding answers. She felt helpless because she wasn't able to be there for Chris and she believed he cried out for her in his time of need. Those thoughts never waned.

As sad as his death was, my heart also hoped it would remove my sister's desire and thirst for drugs. That didn't happen. It had the opposite effect. I got the sense that my sister was trying to take advantage of the situation based on things I witnessed.

For instance, I received well wishes while over at my mother's house and they asked, "Where is Loraine?"

I called her and she said she was at home and didn't know if she was coming over. I suggested she come over because our mother needed her. We all needed her to be there to grieve together as a family. She never came. I went to her place to see how she was doing. Once there, I noticed she was receiving guests as well. She had people donate money via a pickle bucket for Chris' "funeral fund." What took place shocked me, and I also found it to be disrespectful to his memory. Besides, my mother had a burial policy on Chris; there wasn't any need for anything additional.

There was another time when she called the homicide division and gave the detectives a hard time about some cash that was found on Chris' body during the investigation. They did not release the money to the family. Willie spoke with her to address her actions. Everyone understood her pain and the fact that she didn't know how to articulate it, but it wasn't until that time that the reality revealed my sister to be a sick person. She became someone we no longer recognized.

As for me and my brothers, all of our responses were different. My reaction to Chris' death was more polarizing because of the senselessness and level of disrespect.

During the week leading up to the funeral, I met my brother at the hotel by the airport where he worked off duty. "Sarge," as people called him in certain circles, always dressed nice in his uniform. Everything was always on point. He wanted to make sure he represented himself, LRPD, and our family name, as best as he could at all times. He parlayed that appearance and demeanor into being well-respected in the community.

The thought of us having to bury our nephew pissed me off tremendously. That should not happen. We should have gone before him. My brother was always a good listener, and he listened as my rant turned to anger. I was furious at the thought that our own cousin had a hand in Chris' death, and I couldn't erase that thought from my mind! I explained to Willie the anger I felt, and I wanted to get back at Omar for what he did to our family.

He asked, "What good would that do?"

Before I gave my response any thought, I replied, "I don't give a damn!" I wanted that coward dead, too! My brother's response was something profound, although I didn't receive it.

He stated, "We would be burying a relative and I will lose a brother to prison."

I responded, "Man, I don't want to hear all that passive non-violent talk!"

He was quick to be humble, and he reminded me that our nephew had shot someone's daughter and pistol whipped someone's son over some marijuana. What was right about that? That rendered me speechless. No, Chris didn't deserve to die in the manner in which he did, but the young lady didn't deserve to get shot. The young man didn't deserve to get beaten within inches of his life. We didn't argue the point because we tried to respect each other's pain. We made it through the night.

CHAPTER 7

A Suit to be Buried In

The time came for us to decide what attire to bury Chris in. The thought was surreal. I recall being there when Chris came into the world, and I was happy as a lark to have a little nephew. I didn't know anything about being an uncle, but I knew I would be the best uncle a guy like him could ever have. Now, here we are at Horn's Men's Store to purchase attire to say our last goodbyes. Not knowing our reason for being there, the salesperson approached us with a smile and asked, "What is the occasion for you all visiting the store today?"

We paused, then we answered the question. We were there to purchase a suit to bury our family member. After we left the store, we discussed another ironic element in this situation. We talked about how ridiculous it was to buy a suit to put it in the ground. I think we were angry and hurt for Chris and his senseless death. After some time, we settled on a nice black suit.

We dropped off my mother at her house and proceeded to the funeral parlor to deliver the suit. Once there, my brother and I decided that we would help the mortician dress Chris' body. That was a hard decision, but I felt it needed to be done in order for me to have closure.

We met with the funeral director in the lobby of the funeral home. He led us back to the dressing room, where they prepare the bodies for viewing. There, I saw Chris stretched out on a cold metal table. It was unthinkable. I never imagined that the last time we touched our nephew would be to dress him to be placed in a casket and into the ground. They draped him in a plastic body suit due to body fluids leaking from the "Y" incision that takes place during the autopsy process. The state crime lab held his body out past the standard time-frame to bury, which resulted in the leakage. The crime lab holds onto a deceased person's body because of homicide for investigative purposes. It usually takes a little over a week to release the body to the family. Because of the late release of Chris' body, which conflicted with scheduling of the services, things went beyond a reasonable or usual time frame to hold a funeral.

Still, he looked peaceful, the way he often looked when he'd sleep hard, because of a long night of hard living. My brother and I talked to him as if he were asleep because he was always a deep sleeper. That was something we joked about as we prepared his clothing. For a split second, we lost sight of where we were and why. Chris had grown to be a big man, but it was all bulk and muscle. We struggled to try to position his body to apply the clothing. As we put on the under garments and slacks, we had to shift his body in a certain manner to pull the slacks up. As we got to the upper body, we realized there wasn't a t-shirt in his belongings. That's when I took my t-shirt off and put it on his lifeless body. We had to lift him in a seated position. I positioned myself behind him, and that's where I saw the gunshot wound in the back of his neck. Anger came over me once again, and it reminded me how chicken shit and cowardly those bastards were, to shoot a man in the back. They were weaklings and could not face him like men, for fear of what would happen if things went south.

    We put on his shirt, tie, and suit jacket. They attached him to the lift to place his lifeless body into his silver casket. His colors were black with silver accents. His siblings would match Chris at the funeral. Reggie would wear a black suit/shirt with a silver tie, the same as Chris, and Katelyn would wear a black dress with silver accented jewelry and a pendant. Once we placed him in the casket, we reflected on his life and asked why. He should not be here. There was nothing we could do about it now.

******

    It was now Friday, and I realized I finally had a good night's sleep. I could get some of the anger and disappointment off my mind. This was the day of the wake and we all wanted to go to the funeral parlor and view Chris' body together. We wanted to make sure things were in order and going according to the family's plan. When I got to the parlor, I asked the funeral director to only allow his immediate family in for viewing. I didn't want anyone else viewing his body before the wake started. Chris looked well and peaceful while he laid in state. My brother and I did a great job, and the family made a great decision to make Chris' homegoing celebration a memorable one. The way everything lined up satisfied us, therefore we left the parlor and had lunch. No one had much of an appetite, but we mustered up enough to put some much needed food on our stomachs. After lunch, we separated to relax and ease our minds.

We met back up at the funeral parlor around 5 p.m. The wake began at 6. My brothers and I devised a plan of action concerning what we would do to ensure the service was dignified. Someone started a rumor that some shady characters would attend to show "respect." Chris affiliated with the Bleeding Streets gang, and we didn't want any signs of disrespect towards our family during our time of grief. We positioned ourselves with Sarge at the door, to greet Chris' gang member friends and to give them specific instructions about what we would and would not tolerate. I positioned myself and my other brother at opposite ends of the casket to keep anyone from placing gang paraphernalia inside. I was prepared for any one of those cowards who I thought had a hand in Chris' murder, to stroll through the door. There wasn't anything in particular I would do, but I would do something. The wake went according to the plan outlined by the family and funeral directors. I wanted to make sure my mother was okay, and I didn't care to compound her grief by acting out.

The wake was over, but I wasn't about to leave until the last person left. I didn't want Chris' body left alone around people I didn't know or trust. We departed the mortuary and went back to my mother's house for the rest of the evening. The homegoing celebration was the next day. This will be the time when it all became final.

CHAPTER 8

The Last Mile of the Way

This is it. The last mile of the way! It was a beautiful, warm, Saturday morning when I got up and prepared for the services. I didn't get much sleep last night, and I could assume the same for the rest of the family. I stayed at my brother's house because I didn't want my mother to see the anger built up inside of me. She didn't need any extra stress during this time. The funeral directors planned to pick up the family from Sarge's house. The mood was somber. No one was in a light mood. My brother and I often laughed and cut up, but now he was a different person. I could see the hurt on his face. In crises or difficult times, he'd always be the one to think critically through situations and circumstances. I was certain of the helpless feeling he grappled with. He couldn't save our nephew from the streets, no matter how hard he tried. After countless hours of deep thought, I concluded there wasn't much any of us could have done to save Chris. He made his mind up and that's what he was going to do, even if it cost him his life. The streets were where he wanted to be.

Everyone finally arrived at my brother's house to be transported to the church. My mother tried to hold it together, but you could tell she was off kilter. She's always been a rock, a strong black woman. Now she was vulnerable because she lost her grandson and she was overwhelmed with grief. It was like a bad dream she could not shake. My sister looked well, but I could still sense the hurt she experienced. She also felt guilty for not being around for Chris and his siblings. But who was judging her or anyone else on this day? This wasn't the time to pass judgment. We came together as a family to send our son, grandson, brother, and nephew, to his final resting place. Reggie and Katelyn were okay, but could not outmaneuver death. They wanted to take out their grief and anger on the ones responsible for this day. My other sister and brothers did well and wanted to make sure they were strong and upright for the rest of the family.

The family cars arrived on schedule, escorted by the Little Rock Police Department's funeral detail. That was a designation typically reserved for fallen officers, but they were gracious enough to provide escort as a courtesy to my brother. The family loaded into the cars for a normal 15-minute ride to Antioch Baptist Church in College Station. It seemed like it took an eternity to get there. It was a quiet and slow excursion through the neighborhood, then onto the freeway. If we had spoken words during that time, we all would have broken down in tears. Everyone remained silent until we arrived.

It was a nice turnout for Chris' homegoing services. We entered the church in pairs until we filled the family section of the sanctuary. The casket was open, and some people were already viewing his body. I watched everyone as they passed by. I tried to determine if anyone who had a hand in his murder would come to the funeral to check out their work. My mind raced all over the place. *Was it this guy? Was it that guy? Could it have been that female who is adding extra theatrics to her grieving? Were they there to give Chris a final "screw you?"* I was ready to pounce on whatever my mind told me. My head was on a swivel, and my mind was all over the place.

The service started on time, as requested by my mother. The choir sang a few selections chosen by the family; "New Life" by John P. Kee, "Just for Me" by Donnie McClurkin, and "My Life is in Your Hands" by Kirk Franklin. A few close friends spoke kind and encouraging words about growing up with Chris. Someone read words of resolution which would also go into the church's archives. Some of his junior high teachers and coaches spoke about his friendly character. They all said he had a great disposition. As they spoke, I asked myself: *Where in the hell did he go wrong?* It only compounded my anger once again.

It was now time for the Bishop to eulogize Chris. He wanted to make this a special one for my mother, sister, and the rest of the family. They brought all of us up in this church. My mother was an usher on the senior usher board. My sister was a member of the adult choir. The Bishop spoke well of Chris and his upbringing as he delved into his sermon. As he brought his message to a close, he offered the family words of encouragement. But when he spoke, he recited a Scripture while he looked at me. I thought he'd turn away and focus on the congregation, but he continued to look at me as he recited, "for this anger endureth but a moment; in his favor is life: weeping may endure for a night, but joy cometh in the morning...But unto thee have I cried, O LORD and in the morning shall my prayer prevent thee."

I again asked myself, *Why in the hell is he looking at me? Who told him about how pissed off I was? Did my mother share with him my thoughts of revenge?*

He concluded his sermon and called for the funeral directors to come and receive the body. As they prepared to exit the church, the choir sang, "Goin' up Yonder." The finality hit home for me as I became emotional. I had my sunglasses handy, and I put them on as I exited the church and looked straight ahead. We accounted for everybody and headed to the cemetery for Chris' final resting place. It had become hot by the time we left the church. We arrived at the cemetery, and I noticed that the funeral directors didn't have a canopy over the gravesite. That was concerning to me because I knew my mother wouldn't be able to withstand that heat bearing down for an extended period.

Out of respect for the family, the Bishop tried to make the committal service as brief as possible, as I hoped he would. As he spoke, four dusty looking guys walked up with some 40 oz. beer bottles. They looked rough and worth paying attention to, but I didn't put too much thought into them being there. But then, they approached the casket and poured beer on it and flashed gang signs. As I got ready to confront them, my mother grabbed me by the arm and whispered, "I've already lost Chris to foolishness. I don't want to lose you to the same. Let them pour all the beer they want on that casket. It's not going to hurt Chris, nor bring him back." Chris was gone forever!

CHAPTER 9

Back to Life

We held the repast at my brother's house, because it was more spacious to accommodate the volume of people in attendance. My mother didn't feel up to coming over. She went home to get some much needed rest. I knew she didn't feel like entertaining anyone. She wanted her alone time. I stayed at Willie's house for a little while, but later went to my mother's house to be with her. There were a few people at her house, and some others came by later.

We sat on the front porch, talked and reminisced. She told me she had no actual memory of Chris' services. She said everything was a blur. I never told her I felt the same way. There was so much going on and a lot to deal with. As much as I wanted to be there for everyone, I had to prepare to go back to Dallas the following day. We continued to receive guests until late in the evening, and my mother eventually went to bed for the night.

I went back to my brother's house to do the same. This entire ordeal drained me of every emotion I had. We don't know what we can handle until it's time to handle it. We all had to get back to our respective lives. Chris' death changed all our lives in different ways, because we all had our own relationship with him. We wanted to watch over each other while allowing space to grieve in our own individual way. That wasn't easy to do.

In the weeks following the funeral, my mother wanted answers from the homicide detective working the case. His name was Detective Matthew Alexander. Detective Alexander was a 30-year veteran of the Little Rock Police Department. He was born and raised in the College Station community and knew my mother and family well. He was also one of my brother's colleagues on the force, and he assured my mother that he would work hard to solve the case.

My father, Odell, and his brother, Moses, were close. They did almost everything together. All that changed after Chris' murder. My father wasn't angry at his brother for what his son did to his grandson, but there was something he wasn't able to articulate. They didn't have any contentious words, but my father let him know how he felt about what he knew. One thing for certain, my dad no longer considered his nephew as family.

You could tell he wasn't himself. Chris' death would have been hard under different circumstances, but it was extra hard to take knowing family had a hand in it. Time didn't sit still after the murder. We were assertive with the homicide detective and pressed for answers. The police did not satisfy my concerns that they had put forth the resources to get to the bottom of the case. I sensed their sentiments were "another young black male murdered by gun violence," and that's par for the course in Little Rock. It would have been different had the victim been white, and from the more affluent part of town. It would have made the news cycle on repeat, with a sizable reward for information. Not for Chris' murder, though.

They hid the article written about him in the middle section of the whole newspaper. His case went cold, and the detectives no longer had anything to offer in terms of updates. I felt that if nothing landed in their laps, they damn sure would not look for anything. The police still investigated Chris' murder because they needed to apply due diligence to arrive at their own conclusion. Witnesses that could have cracked the case, refused to talk to them. People who knew firsthand what happened, shared that information with people close to our family. Until they spoke up, the investigators only considered it "hearsay."

I called my mother almost daily, and she wasn't as upbeat as she used to be. She slept a lot during the latter parts of the day. She also fought hard to strike up a conversation, although she tried her best. I could say something funny and make her laugh a little, but I could tell she struggled to mask her grief.

I also visited Little Rock in the months after the murder, including during Thanksgiving and Christmas. The sight of my mother's pained expression saddened me even more. I later realized it broke her heart into pieces. Shattered! No parent or grandparent should bury their child or grandchild. I sensed that my mother was giving up on life. I wished there was something I could do to help her find joy again. However, she would never find joy for the remainder of her days on earth.

******

It was now the winter of 2003, and we were no closer to finding out the truth than we were in the beginning. Plenty of people came around and told my sister, niece, and nephew, what they claimed to know or what they heard. But not one of them would go to my brother or contact the homicide detective. They feared potential retaliation from Omar. They didn't trust the police to protect them, therefore they kept quiet with their information. My mother and my sister told them to never come back around since they didn't want to help.

They both resigned themselves to the fact that Chris' death would go unsolved, and to be truthful, I felt the same way. We also directed that sentiment towards the so-called friends of Chris and our family. They showed their true colors during our time of need. I haven't spoken to them since.

I traveled to Little Rock in February to visit my mother. It was Chris' birthday month, and I went in his honor. I knew there wouldn't be a celebration, but I felt she needed me there. It snowed that weekend and my mother was relaxing in her living room when I arrived. The rest of the family was there as well, and it delighted her to see us. She joked and acted like her old self. I bought a new digital camera and brought it with me. I had never taken it out of the box and toyed around with it while I was there. She suggested I take some photos of her. At first, she wore what the old folk called a "duster." When it came time to take the photos, she went into her room and got a fur coat and one of her "church" hats to wear for the shoot. We weren't able to view the photos at the time because of some technical issues, but we had a lot of laughs while we took them. I was happy that I could get some photos of my mother as she smiled once again. We never talked about the things we loved about Chris. Considering Chris' passing, she felt it important to never talk about it for fear of losing it. The great photographer, Robert Frank, once said, "Things move on, time passes, people go die or go away. Sometimes they don't come back. Only photos remain."

My mother passed away a month later, on Monday, March 10, at 9:30 a.m. She was a young, heartbroken, 64 year-old-woman. The news of her passing was another blow to the family, as we still grieved and tried to process Chris' death. We talked on the phone the night before, and she was having a great time with my siblings and her surviving grandkids.

The morning of Mom's passing, Katelyn, was getting ready for school and Mom appeared to be fine. Katelyn got dressed, left the house, and headed to the bus stop. She said Mom was awake, eating breakfast, and watching television when she left. She told Katelyn to have a great day at school. Katelyn was away from the house for about 15 minutes, when she realized she left her homework. By the time she made it back to the house, she walked in the door to find my mother lying on the floor, unresponsive. Katelyn was unprepared for what she walked into. She called 911. The dispatcher asked the standard probing questions and discovered that Katelyn didn't know how to administer first aid. She tried to coach her to perform CPR until EMS arrived, but shock and grief overwhelmed her. Her efforts were not effective. The ambulance arrived within minutes of being dispatched. They immediately treated my mother in her living room. Whenever a 911 call comes through, it goes to a dispatch center. When available, police officers will respond to ambulance calls. Not only can they assist Emergency Medical Services as they performed their duties, they can also help provide care and comfort to those in need.

Willie was the officer who took that call on that fateful day. Being a trained professional on the force, he's had his fair share of eventful calls. This call was different. The address where he grew up, 2303 Howard Street, came through his radio. He rushed to the location to find the first responders administering chest compressions to our mother as they escorted her out of the house on a gurney. Willie could see she was in distress by the manner of which they provided treatment. According to him, her eyes were open, and he knew she was no longer with us. I couldn't imagine what my niece and brother went through during that time. I know that they both felt a sense of helplessness once again.

I never asked my niece about it, but I discussed that day with my brother. He said he knew it was our mother when he heard the address over his radio, and that the ambulance crew worked hard to save her, but it was too late. He followed the ambulance to University Hospital to make proper identification. Her doctor diagnosed her with congestive heart failure quite some time ago, but we believe she died of a broken heart. She never got back to her old self after Chris' murder and never got over it. Almost everything about preparing for her funeral and the actual service, were a blur to me, because I found myself again consumed with that same rage I had with Chris' death. In essence, the same cousin who had a hand in my nephew's murder now had a hand in my mother's death. Her sorrow and depression resulted from what he did.

People often think that the ones who die from homicides are the only victims of the crime. That's far from the truth. The survivors, the ones left to pick up the pieces, are victims as well.

CHAPTER 10

A Cold Beer and a Chew

Our family now had to wrestle with the fact that we've lost our nephew and mother—the matriarch of the family—both in a span of eight months. That's a hard pill to swallow. Time has this funny habit of waiting for no one. Days turned into months. Months turned into years. As time went on, I came to realize that the police weren't interested in solving Chris' murder.

The homicides continued to pile up, and it was all black on black crime. The homicide team, lead by Detective Matthew Alexander, would allow some murders to cancel themselves out. When either of us would check on the status with him, the answer would always be, "We are still working leads."

Then, one day out of the blue, the police announced they had solved Chris's murder. The authorities reported a drive-by shooting at a car wash on East 9th Street, in the old historical East End community, that left one person dead and two others wounded. The authorities concluded the drive-by murder on East 9th Street was in retaliation for Chris' murder, because the person who died was related to Omar and Doby. The detectives figured that someone affiliated with Chris' gang plotted revenge for his murder.

They found it too coincidental for the murdered person to be related to Omar and Doby, because the streets were saying Chris killed Doby and Omar had Chris killed. They suspected the person killed in this shooting, shot Chris. Case closed.

Several months after my mother's passing, I made another commute to Little Rock. As I traveled through the city, I stopped by my mother's house to sit on the porch and feel her presence. When I pulled up, my dad was cutting the lawn.

I got out of the car and asked, "What's going on? Why are you cutting her grass? "

He said he'd been maintaining the lawn ever since she passed. I wanted to know more about what he felt.

I asked, "Would you like a cold beer?"

He said, "Sure," and asked for the Stag brand.

That was the only beer I've ever known him to drink. I left to get some beer to quench his thirst, and my thirst for what was on his mind. I went to Round-A-Bout Liquor Store at the intersection of Roosevelt Road and MLK Drive.

That was the store my dad went to for his favorite beer, because he always knew they had it in stock. I bought a six pack of Stag beer and a can of Kodiak chewing tobacco for good measure. That was his choice of chew, as well.

When I got back to the house, we sat on the porch and talked. I didn't ask about anything in particular. My father opened up about how he felt regarding what happened to Chris. He spoke about how he despised Omar, and always knew he was trouble. He said he shared his concerns with Chris when he first heard he was hanging around him.

My father confessed that Omar's parents didn't raise them right in terms of direction and discipline. They could run the streets of College Station, unsupervised and with reckless abandon. Their mother didn't work, and Uncle Moses always worked odd jobs with my father. Their parents both drank to excess and fought all the time. The children, all nine of them, were a witness to the violence and brutality. Their household was dysfunctional.

Omar never finished school and developed a bad reputation among the teachers and staff at the Pulaski County School District. His mother was always sick, but their grandmother provided what little discipline she could muster. The rest of his siblings were delinquents as well, but they weren't as bad as him.

My dad kept his distance from them as they grew up. The conversation we had shocked me, but I was pleased. That's the first time we took the time to sit and talk about substantive things. He was candid, and he articulated how he felt about everything that happened over the past few months. But there was one profound element that stood out the most.

My father told me, "I love you."

Hearing those three words blew me away that day because he had never said those words to me, and I can't recall a time where my siblings said he'd told them, "I love you." Although our father hadn't been all that he could have been to us, and for us, I developed a newfound desire to have more dialogue with him, perhaps over another cold beer.

******

Over the years, we sadly lost aunts, uncles, and cousins. As we gathered to lay them to rest, the consistent attitude was there would be no fellowshipping with that side of the family. I wasn't trying to sit anywhere close to any of them, in the family section of whichever sanctuary we were in. I didn't care to break bread with them at any repast or gathering. If I saw them talking to other relatives I was preparing to speak with, I would go the other way. Some of my siblings would try to encourage me to "let it go."

They said, "You would have to forgive," because that would be best for me. Says who? No! I will not let it go, nor will I ever forgive! I had nothing for any of them. I felt nothing for any of them. I don't claim them as any family of mine. They meant nothing to me, and I was okay with that.

My father's and stepmother's health deteriorated along with his relationship with Uncle Moses. His decline was noticeable, but he wouldn't speak about it. When asked, he would always say, "I'm fine."

My siblings visited with him and would call me so we could talk as well. I would see him whenever I came to town. He would always bring up Chris and how pissed he was about what happened to him. When I asked him about my uncle, he would say he hadn't spoken to him in a while. I know he loved his brother, and his brother loved him as well. It's like neither one of them could express themselves to each other. I still checked on them both to make sure they didn't stray any further from each other.

My stepmother passed away at home on March 8, 2013. She'd become ill and wasn't able to recover. My dad was sad and alone. We sensed that he would decline further if we didn't step in and see what we could do to help him. He was at a crossroads of sorts. He didn't know the first thing to do, therefore he called my oldest sister. She coordinated with my brother and they went over to offer support.

They helped my stepmother's children make the funeral arrangements. Once they scheduled the funeral, I made it back to Little Rock to attend the services. This was my stepmother's celebration of life and homegoing services, and all about honoring her. I still wasn't able to ignore the fact that I would be in the same church with the ones I couldn't stand being around.

As the pastor acknowledged my father and the surviving family members, my eyes found "them" on the other side of the church. I tuned out the pastor's message and wondered, *What if? What if I could avenge Chris' murder and not get caught. How would I carry it out? Would I tell anyone? Am I capable of such a dastardly deed? What is my dad thinking at the moment?*

My father seemed empty. Before I realized it, the pallbearers had prepared to wheel the casket out of the church. As we exited, my brother extended his hand to one of those cousins, and he got rebuffed. Once I saw that, I was ready to fight. To me, that was the ultimate sign of disrespect, and I wasn't about to have it. My brother talked me off that ledge. He said that mess did not bother him, but it bothered me. I don't believe in "killing them with kindness!" To hell with them all! I meant that in my spirit!

CHAPTER 11

Brothers

Another family member went on to glory, and we laid her to rest. It was time again to be in the same space as "them." That's how I regarded certain members of my family, or my cousins, when other family members wanted to be messy. My dad now lived with extended family, including some of his step grandchildren. That arrangement seemed okay in the beginning, but it turned into something concerning.

During a random visit by my brother, he noticed Dad was in a bedroom in the back of the house and there wasn't any food in the fridge.

He asked my dad, "What's going on?"

He responded, "I don't know all the folks who come in and out of the house, and none of them have jobs." My brother figured if they didn't have jobs, they had no financial contributions to offer on the utilities. We decided that either they had to go, or Dad had to go. Whichever way, we would not help him pay his rent while they lived there as well. It was time for them to step up.

That didn't happen, and Dad moved in with my brother. By this time, his diabetic condition worsened to where he had to have two toes amputated. That was the start of more to come in terms of his health. The next surgery was to amputate half of his right foot. Following that was a below-the-knee, right leg amputation. Besides diabetes, he had an aggressive infection that the doctors could not control. He was in and out of the hospital, and had multiple nurses through home health services in between hospital stays.

Through it all, we made him comfortable in the confines of my brother's house. Aside from his health, he wanted for nothing. He ate the right foods and had meals prepared for him daily. With Dad now staying with my brother, it allowed great opportunities for the rest of the family to visit with him at anytime. He loved spending time with his children and grandchildren, especially Katelyn's daughter, Kloe, who he referred to as "Klora." As happy as he was to have them all around him, he would always mention that Chris was missing. He wished Chris was with all of us, and he wished he knew what happened that terrible night.

On the other side of town, in the downtown area, Uncle Moses spoke of how much he missed his brother and the talks they used to have. What he knew surrounding Chris' murder upset and bothered him. We encouraged him to get on the phone and speak with his brother.

One day he did, and they filled their conversation with joy. They called each other more freely, without hesitation.

When I came to town and visited family, I would always ask Dad, "Have you spoken to your brother?"

He was happy to report that he had. Dad was always in an upbeat mood. He didn't complain about much, but when he did, it was because he missed his oldest grandson.

With the passing of time, Dad's health deteriorated at a rapid pace. The infection came back more aggressively. He went into the hospital on multiple occasions. In due course, and after countless diagnostic testing, the doctor revealed that the cause of his infections was improper healing of his leg amputation.

In March 2016, the doctors advised he needed to have another surgery to remove the affected area of the same leg that was amputated. That news was rather soul-crushing to him. The doctors were candid when they advised that he needed surgery or the infection could kill him. After a family meeting, he decided he would not have another surgery.

He stated, "I'm tired of them cutting on me. If it's the Good Lord's will to take me home, so be it."

True to the doctor's prognosis, his condition worsened and my brother had a challenge providing care to him in the home while he tried to work. It was difficult for the rest of the siblings as well, because no one could provide around-the-clock care for him. Everyone worked and had their families to take care of as well. The care he needed would be better if he were in a care facility.

It was heartbreaking to take this news to Dad. He agreed to it, but I knew he didn't want to go. After all the paperwork and insurance information was provided, Dad moved into room # 21A of the Comfort Keepers Skilled Nursing Facility around the middle of April. He settled in, and appeared to do well.

For the first few weeks, my siblings visited with him daily. This care plan was important because these visitations could clue us into any signs of declining mental cognition, health, or mobility. It was also important because it would give us a chance to check up on my dad's happiness and health, and to make sure nothing has changed to concern us since the last time one of them visited with Dad. He enjoyed the visits, but they could see a decline in him. His conversations became limited, and he stopped eating. It became concerning, and we sensed he was about to give up. Most of the time, he slept.

He needed to be comfortable. He was fortunate to have had the time to visit with his brother. They cleared the air between them. Uncle Moses apologized for his son's involvement in Chris' murder. They cried together and hugged one another. That would be their last conversation. Dad passed away in peace on May 9, 2016. He was 81 years old.

As we were preparing funeral arrangements for Dad, we weren't thinking of him as being gone away as his journey had just begun. We thought of him as resting in the loving arms of his Savior. No more suffering. No more grief. I was at peace with that thought. We used the same funeral parlor as my mother and nephew.

I made the excursion from Dallas to Little Rock, as I've done on many occasions. This time around, my feelings were a different kind of sadness. I was more reflective of his complicated life. I always wondered what was on his mind because he always seemed so laid back. He was not quick to anger or act. His demeanor was identical to that of my oldest brother, whose temperament is misdirected as if to evade any conversation that's akin to matters of the heart, particularly those that are emotionally based. I often believed his lack of conversation was his way of not wanting to address issues that might lead in the direction of responsibility. Not only for himself but also those of us who expected him to.

How did he feel knowing that a strong black woman raised his children? He benefited from a woman who refused to say a negative word about him around the children. She made sure we respected him, despite not deserving it. She extended grace to him, even though he married another woman and raised her children and grandchildren. My mother never took him to court for the child support she could, without a doubt, use. My mother even had it written in her last will and testament for us to take care of him if he ever fell on hard times or got too sick to take care of himself. I guess she foresaw what was to come regarding him and wanted to make sure he was in good hands. To know all of what my mother had to sacrifice to pick up the slack for him must have weighed on his mind through the years.

Dad's wake was on Friday, May 13, at the funeral parlor. People packed it to capacity, with overflow in the common area. A lot of the folks who paid their respects included our friends, coworkers, and others from the neighborhood who knew Dad and other family and friends. He had three remaining siblings who were there. As I made my rounds to thank those who came to pay respects, I laid eyes on my uncle.

He looked frail and carried a portable oxygen tank. I never realized he was on oxygen because no one had mentioned it to me. I was happy to see him. He stood next to a few of his children I didn't care to speak to. I had no interest or intention of acknowledging them or speaking to them. My uncle said he got the chance to speak with my dad and they both said the things that needed to be said. Uncle Moses said, "The biggest mistake we make in life is thinking we have time."

We buried my father the following day. Uncle Moses refused to enter the church for the funeral. He opted to remain outside until we were ready to head to the cemetery for the committal service. He never explained why he chose not to go in, and I never asked.

With Dad's passing, we made every attempt to remain in contact with our uncle. He shuffled back and forth from his apartment in the high rise to his daughter's house. When he was in his own apartment, we could speak at ease. When he was over at his daughter's house, she wouldn't allow him to have access to his cell phone, therefore, we didn't speak during those times. His health failed as well, and it forced him to stay with his daughters throughout. They would shuffle him from house to house and keep him shielded from us. We could not reach him on his cell phone and didn't know how he was doing or how ill he had become.

After several months of living with his daughters, they admitted him into the hospital for unknown reasons. He remained in the hospital for three months, and later moved to hospice care once they decided he wouldn't survive the next six months. His children wouldn't share any information with us concerning his hospitalization. He passed away on April 3, 2019, of unknown causes. I was once again back on the road to Little Rock to pay my final respects to one of my favorite uncles. As much as I respected him and wanted to honor him, I had no intentions on making nice with his children. This time, I attended my uncle's wake and funeral, but I didn't go to the cemetery. It was a rainy and muggy day, and I didn't feel up to being wet *and* despising the sight of his children. As petty as that is, I didn't care.

There was a repast, but they did not invite us to it and that was fine with me. His children had it at an undisclosed location. The other cousins and I got together and had a fish fry in honor of our beloved uncle. It ended up turning into a mini reunion of sorts. We all had a great time, despite the circumstances.

CHAPTER 12

Where Do We Go From Here?

Since Chris, my mother, father, cousins, aunts, and uncles, passed, I haven't had any contact with the friends who didn't want to help to solve Chris' case. I'm still in constant contact with my stepmother's children and some of her grandkids. They are some of the nicest people I've had the pleasure of knowing. I feel these people loved my father as if he were blood related. I still have cousins and other family members I am in contact with, as well as some cousins from Uncle Moses, but not the ones who either had a hand in Chris' murder, or who are complicit. They know who they are, and I have no intentions of ever speaking to them again. Through the years, our family has endured many tragedies and heartfelt losses. As life goes on and loved ones pass away, we must continue to grieve and mourn separately.

It's been difficult to come together as one family. It might be because certain wounds are too deep to heal. Maybe it's because the ones who used to make sure we all got along and united as a family are no longer with us. Or maybe the desire to be family no longer exists. While the former is true, I refuse to embrace the latter. I am inclined to believe that we must, regardless of how painful it may be, address the unresolved trauma that has thrived in the fabric of our family. A lot of trauma continues to occupy my mind and the minds of people I am supposed to love and respect.

Our African American experience has resulted in a lot of pain and suffering for not only my family and relatives, but for the entire country of individuals who look like me. How do we address this unresolved trauma? It is apparent that I have allowed my belief in what happened to my nephew to affect my feelings toward a segment of my relatives. Those feelings directed my thoughts about them, which initiated how I reacted and responded to them.

Here are a few questions to consider: What is crucial for the African American culture to know? First, we must answer the question, what is trauma? Then we must answer, where does trauma come from? We must also answer, what does trauma look like and how does it affect how we behave and react to situations? More importantly, the question we must answer is, how do we heal?

We all have stumbled in our efforts to address issues within our families; with our mothers, fathers, sisters, and brothers. However, I know we can do it. I can only imagine the "trauma bonding" that takes place when individuals share their unresolved traumatic experiences that have consumed them for most of their lives. Having candid, careful, and concerned conversations is not easy, nor are they comfortable. The unpleasantness of this type of discussion can happen if it derives from a place called love. We will continue to search for the answers.

One of a few things I can surmise from the behaviors of my father is fatherlessness. We can say the same for my nephew, my cousin, his nephew, and many other young black men who feel wayward and hopeless. Although my father's father was present in his life, it doesn't automatically translate into guidance.

When my brothers and I were young, I remember a particular situation like it happened yesterday. My parents divorced when I was a toddler, and I had no recollection of him ever being in the household. We lived in the projects of Granite Mountain. Staring out the window of # 26 Burbank Lane, I recall my brother's fingers pressed hard against the cheap window pane as he eagerly waited for our father's car to round the corner and pick us up for the weekend. My brother's position in that window was nothing new, as we all had assumed that position at one point or another, and always experienced the same result…a no show!

It wasn't until our teenage years that we reflected on why our mother was always in the background, yelling at us to get away from the window. I never understood the harm in us watching and waiting for our "daddy" to come and pick us up. Then it hit us! We had an epiphany, although we were too young to understand what that word meant. Our mother hurt for us because she knew he would not come. She wasn't angry at us for looking out the window while we waited for his arrival.

Unfortunately, even today, in our adult lives, black fathers still do not "show up!" They do not show up for birth, graduation, and recently, one didn't show up for his son's funeral! These disappearing acts of fathers have placed some of them in a category close to the famous magician David Copperfield. Because I can relate to the feeling of being let down, or even lied to for no reason than to lie, it has allowed me to operate through a vein of empathy when relating to the trauma connected to absentee fathers.

One thing we knew we needed then, and black boys still need now, is what I refer to as the three "Ps:" Presence, Provision, and Praise. When we as fathers are not present, then there is no communication. There is no access. A lot can go wrong. Presence is important. It means you are alive and you are somewhere. However, "present" can also mean or indicate that you are here for me right now. If we are to save our children, we must be present for them to look up to. We must be present to provide them with the love and value they crave. If we don't give them that, then the "go to" response is anger and pain.

My brother, Sgt. Willie Davis, is a police officer and the coordinator of a mentoring program in Little Rock, Arkansas. They named the mentoring program, "Our Kids Program." The O.K. Program is a law enforcement based mentoring program for black men and boys. Black police officers lead it throughout certain cities, across the country. Fatherlessness is something that the participants are passionate about. In his calling as a mentor, he has witnessed black males entering through the doors of the O.K. Program with a lack of fathering. When the mentees witness or experience a strong male figure, something positive takes place. They see themselves in a positive light. Most social ills that they deal with are directly or indirectly, related to fatherlessness. Young men, who grow up in homes without fathers, are twice as likely to end up in jail, as those who come from traditional two-parent households.

It pains my heart to imagine the amount of trauma our children must endure daily. In most cases, our kids live in houses where death knocks on the front door and pain creeps in through the back door.

I'm reminded of a time in 2008 when my brother first worked with the O.K. Program. One benefit of the mentees of the program consisted of home visits. The facilitator could have visibility regarding the mentee's living conditions.

In the mentoring arena, there are moments when you become overwhelmed with the constant appearance of hopelessness, coupled with the lack of parental involvement. There was an instance where Willie visited a home of a high school student enrolled in the program.

On this day, Willie found his resolve tested and strengthened. He spoke to the grandmother of the student by phone, and she asked him to visit with the young man. My brother knew this student's mother was alive, however he had not met her.

However, the grandmother mentioned to her daughter that her son had a mentor with the O.K. Program. When he arrived at the home, there were three grownups sitting along the steps of the front porch. There were two males and one female, who each held thin brown paper bags with tall beverages inside. Be mindful that he is a sergeant with the Little Rock Police Department, and was in full regalia. As he approached them, it allowed him to glance at the top of a can as they walked away. The adults in the mentee's household had no regard for the child's well-being, let alone a uniformed police officer. They didn't conceal their alcohol consumption, but they showed contempt for the effort to pay a home visit. The woman spoke and acknowledged him by his rank and last name. It surprised him because he didn't recognize her. He acknowledged her as he entered the residence that was in disarray. The young student appeared embarrassed as he led my brother to his grandmother's room. My brother thought, *I can't do this!* As he turned the corner into the grandmother's bedroom, there she lay bedridden. She smiled and thanked him for coming. She then informed him that the woman who had spoken to him and walked away was the young man's mother. Willie was furious!

It upset him because of his passion for the plight of the black youth in Little Rock. Making a home visit and contact with a parent who implies they are someone else but later revealed to be a parent who does not show any concern about the child's well-being, will infuriate anyone trying to help the community.

There are several risks that fatherless children face and several that trouble me while supporting the concerns regarding absent fathers. According to the National Principals Association Report on the State of High Schools:

- 70% of juveniles in state operated institutions come from fatherless homes (Source: U.S. Department of Justice).

- 71% of all high school dropouts come from fatherless homes (Source: National Principals Association Report on the State of High Schools).
- 85% of all youth sitting in prison grew up in a fatherless home (Source: Fulton Co. Georgia Jail populations, Texas Department of Corrections).

These numbers tell a truth that many don't realize, or fail to accept. There is, however, another side to this dilemma. For us, our father was not present or active in our lives and he did not teach us "how to be a man." Therefore, our beliefs about what a father should be had its basis in what we lacked as a child. For sure, that lack did not come from our mother. She stepped up and did what some would deem impossible. She did what was uncomfortable and abnormal, and she handled her business. By observing our friends who came from two-parent households, we thought being a father meant living with your children, paying bills, and buying toys.

We did not grasp, nor did we understand, the social, emotional, and mental components of being a father until we became fathers. My brother was a high school senior and traumatized at the reality of becoming a father. That was traumatizing to both parents-to-be. In countless conversations with my brother, there was one thing he was certain of. His little girl would not have to peek out of a window with reluctant hope that he might show up. He was always excited to hear her little feet run to the door when he rang the doorbell at her grandmother's house. We both believe and know that choosing to be a responsible father was pivotal to her emotional and personal development.

Reconciling our differences with our father regarding his absenteeism was not for us. But something happened. He started to verbalize his love for my brother. We had never heard it before, and my brother was 50 when he first heard it. He's 56 now. As mentioned earlier, our father passed away in 2016. As my brother reflected on our father's life after his passing, something profound happened. He realized our father had done more for us than we ever thought. He showed us what we did not want to be, and that was an absentee father!

Black boys continue to struggle with unresolved emotions and negative feelings toward the man who bear the responsibility for being a father to them. This has become a generational problem for black men and boys. I believe our black boys want and need love from their fathers or another man he loves and respects. All men have a responsibility to extend that love to a young boy who does not have it. This is critical if we have any hope of changing today's society. We did not get into this condition overnight, and we will not get out of it overnight. We have work to do. If you are like me, you become weary of watching the six o'clock news where one black male is dead, and another is on his way to jail. This work will take a full, all out community effort from churches, schools, local business owners, and responsible God-fearing black men. Mental Health advocacy is a must. Police departments need to integrate a trauma lens into designing strategies to reduce violence. They should institute trauma informed training for all police officers. Parents must stop being lenient and not correcting mistakes. There have been heart-wrenching calls from mothers who call the mentors with their heart in their hands, pleading for them to allow their 20-something-year-old "babies" to turn themselves in to the authorities. The mothers feared that if this law enforcement officer didn't take their sons into custody, other police officers would kill them. They had each committed homicides. During this officer's 28-year career in law enforcement, that scenario happened three times. One of the "babies" still had the weapon in his possession. Their fathers... no show!

Finally, if we continue to neglect the teaching and upbringing of our youth, we will become a nation on the decline. If we refuse to engage them, we will for sure lose control of them. India Arie said it best in a song titled, "Better People." She states, "There is certain information that you can only get in conversation when young people talk to old people, it would make us a better people all around."

We must end this love affair America has with violence and crime. If we can't or won't do this, then we will continue to kick the can down the road towards prisons, while whistling past graveyards.

About The Author

Gregory Davis was born in Little Rock, in the beautiful natural state of Arkansas. He received his education at The University of Central Arkansas. He is employed in the medical field as a Corporate Compliance Analyst in Dallas, TX.

He lives and works out of his home in the Dallas/Fort Worth area. Gregory considers family to be the most important to him. When not spending quality time with family and friends, you will always find him reading some material for content for his next piece. Be on the lookout for something intriguing, comical, suspenseful, or what have you. You will never know what you will get from his busy mind.